The Dirt on Dirt

By **Paulette Bourgeois**
With **Kathy Vanderlinden**

Illustrated by **Martha Newbigging**

Kids Can Press

Kids Can Press acknowledges the financial support of the Government of Ontario, through the Ontario Media Development Corporation's Ontario Book Initiative; the Ontario Arts Council; the Canada Council for the Arts; and the Government of Canada, through the BPIDP, for our publishing activity.

Published in Canada by
Kids Can Press Ltd.
29 Birch Avenue
Toronto, ON M4V 1E2

Published in the U.S. by
Kids Can Press Ltd.
2250 Military Road
Tonawanda, NY 14150

www.kidscanpress.com
Adapted by Kathy Vanderlinden from *The Amazing Dirt Book* by Paulette Bourgeois.

Edited by Kathy Vanderlinden
Designed by Julia Naimska
Printed and bound in Singapore

The hardcover edition of this book is smyth sewn casebound.
The paperback edition of this book is limp sewn with a drawn-on cover.

CM 08 0 9 8 7 6 5 4 3 2
CM PA 08 0 9 8 7 6 5 4 3 2 1

Library and Archives Canada Cataloguing in Publication

Bourgeois, Paulette
   The dirt on dirt / written by Paulette Bourgeois ; illustrated by Martha Newbigging.

ISBN 978-1-55453-101-1 (bound)
ISBN 978-1-55453-102-8 (pbk.)

1. Soils—Juvenile literature. 2. Soil ecology—Juvenile literature.
I. Newbigging, Martha II. Title.

S591.3.B783 2008   j631.4   C2007-902700-8

Photo Credits
Every reasonable effort has been made to trace ownership of, and give accurate credit to, copyrighted material. Information that would enable the publisher to correct any discrepancies in future editions would be appreciated.

Abbreviations:
t=top; **b**=bottom; **c**=center; **l**=left; **r**=right

All photos are © 2008 JupiterImages Corporation with the following exceptions:
P1: Shutterstock; **P6: (cr)** Hemera; **P15:** Shutterstock; **P30: (tl)** Donna O'Meara, **(b)** Erika Powers; **P31:** Jane Kurisu; **P32:** Hemera; **P34–38:** Shutterstock.

Kids Can Press is a *Corus*™ Entertainment company

Contents

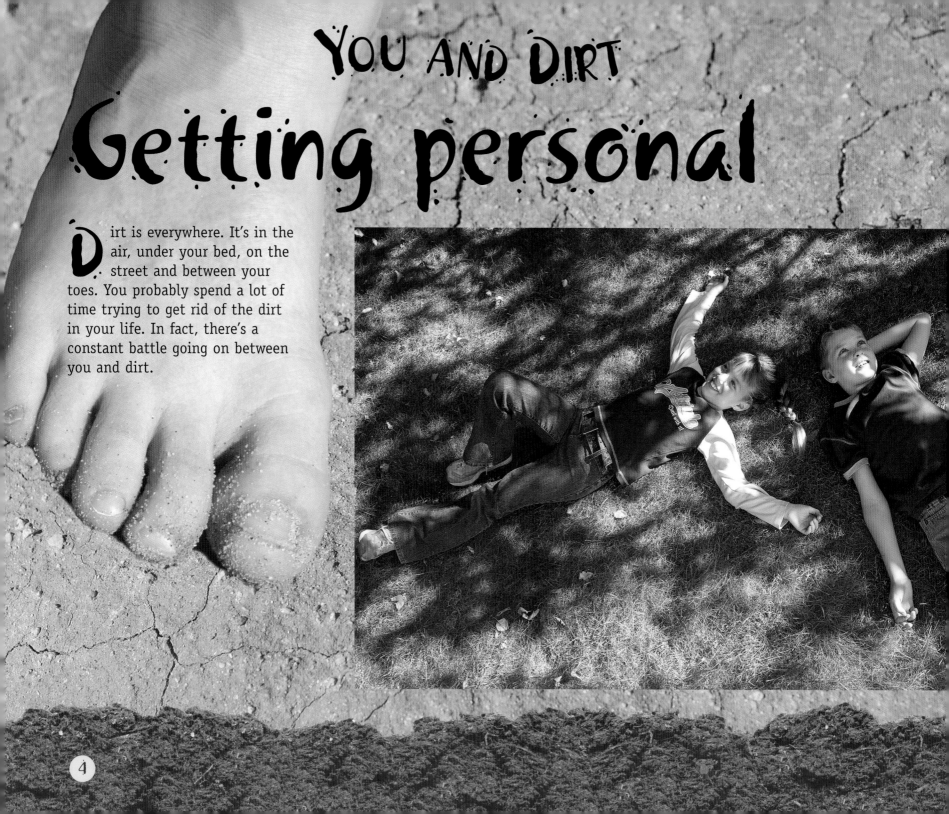

Getting personal

Dirt is everywhere. It's in the air, under your bed, on the street and between your toes. You probably spend a lot of time trying to get rid of the dirt in your life. In fact, there's a constant battle going on between you and dirt.

Let's say you just had a shower. You must be squeaky clean, right? Wrong! The second you step out of the spray, you start getting dirty again. Head to toe, here's where the dirt hides — and how your body tries to fight it off:

• Your scalp makes an oil that lubricates your skin and hair. Dirt clings to the oil.

• Dirt tries to sneak into your ears, but they have a natural dirt protector. Earwax traps the dirt before it reaches your delicate inner ear.

• Grit tries to blow into your eyes, but again your body defends itself. First your eyelashes flap up and down to flick away the dirt. If that fails, your windshield wipers turn on — you blink.

• Take a deep breath of dirty air and your nose goes to work. It's lined with tiny hairs that filter out dirt so it doesn't get into your lungs.

• Sweat gets trapped in your belly button, and lint from your clothes sticks to it. The result: belly-button fluff.

• Your nails are real dirt grabbers. If you scratch a cut or put a dirty fingernail in your mouth, you might be giving dirt, germs and even tiny parasites a free ride into your body. The only solution? Scrub those nails.

• As for how dirt gets between your toes, dirt sticks to wet spots. When your feet sweat, the dirt grabs on.

Warning! Don't read this chapter if you have a weak stomach. There is so much gunk under your nails and so many icky things lurking in dust that you may go crazy cleaning. And if you think water cleans away dirt, read on. Dirt is tough stuff.

Soap up!

You can scrub as long as you like with plain water, but you'll never get yourself really clean. Here's why: Each tiny molecule (particle) of water has a weak electrical charge that makes it attractive to other water molecules. The molecules stick together and can't mix with oil and grease.

To get rid of the dirt, you have to use soap with the water. Soap acts as an emulsifier, allowing water and greasy dirt to mix (see opposite page). It makes the dirt slippery so it loosens its grip on your skin and gets washed away.

Soapless soap

Long ago, the Phoenicians discovered that boiling goat fat, water and ash until the liquids evaporated made a hard, waxy soap. Soap makers have followed a similar recipe ever since.

Soap is wonderful stuff, but it has its drawbacks. It leaves a scum, for one thing. During World War I, the Germans couldn't get fat into the country to make soap. They needed something to wash with, so they invented detergent, a "soapless soap" made from chemicals. To everyone's surprise, detergent worked better than soap. It didn't leave scum, and it wasn't affected by the minerals in hard water. Today's detergents often contain extra ingredients such as bleach and enzymes that boost their cleaning power.

IMPERIAL

POWDERED SOAP
and
LAUNDRY DETERGENT

Mix oil and water

How do soap and detergents work? Try this experiment to find out.

You'll need
- 2 small jars with tight lids
- water
- red food coloring
- cooking oil
- liquid soap or detergent

1 Fill one jar with water. Add two drops of red food coloring and stir. Pour half of the now pink water into the second jar.

2 Fill up each jar with cooking oil. Notice how the liquids separate into two layers, with the oil on top.

3 Add a squirt of soap or detergent to one jar only. Screw both lids on tight.

4 Shake each jar for about five seconds and set it down again. What do you see now?

When you shake the jars, the liquids are thrown together like bumper cars at a fun fair. In the jar without soap, the oil and water eventually separate again into their yellow and pink layers. But in the other jar, the soap doesn't let that happen. Instead, the whole thing becomes a sudsy orange mixture.

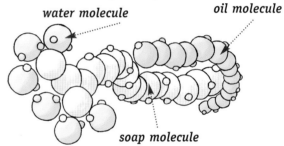

water molecule   *oil molecule*

soap molecule

Oil and water molecules slide off each other, but soap molecules stick to them both. When the molecules mix, one end of a soap molecule grabs water molecules, and the other end grabs oil. That makes it hard for the two liquids to separate. The same thing happens when you have a shower or wash clothes. The soap molecules hold onto the dirt particles until they are rinsed together down the drain.

Mud baths

Have you ever thought of getting dirty to get clean? Sounds backward, but rhinos, pigs and elephants do it all the time. A good wallow in the mud gets rid of ticks and fleas. And when the mud dries hard, it helps protect the animals from the hot sun.

Lots of people love mud baths, too. Every year, for example, tourists flock to the Dead Sea to slather on the smelly, coal-black mud. Under their sun-baked mud coats, bodies warm up and aches and pains melt away. Dead Sea mud is also claimed to cure acne, psoriasis and even wrinkles. What's in the magic mud? A mix of minerals such as feldspar, quartz, calcite and magnesium, and sodium, bromide and chlorine salts.

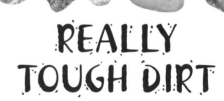

REALLY TOUGH DIRT

Protein dirt (such as blood, egg or milk stains) is hard to clean up. Its molecules are long, tangled chains. You need special enzyme detergents to cut through the chains to loosen them. Enzymes "eat" the dirt much as enzymes in your stomach "eat" your food.

Dirt under your bed

There is some amazing stuff under your bed, and we don't mean the gum wrappers. No matter where you live, you'll find volcanic ash, garden soil, sea salt, car exhaust, flakes of skin, flea eggs, bits of fiber, and grit from bricks and stone — even African sand. There are 300 000 things floating in every cubic foot of air, over, under and around your bed. There are a few *in* your bed, too.

How does African sand get into your bedroom? Sand grains come in different sizes, the largest about 2 mm (0.08 in.). Light breezes roll the middle-sized grains of sand across the desert. When they hit something bigger, they bounce high in the air like acrobats on a circus trampoline. The sand grains spin up to 1000 times per second until they fall back onto the desert. When they land on the tiniest sand grains, those grains go flying in turn. Up to 90 000 000 t (100 000 000 tn.) of these tiny sand grains are sent airborne each year. The hot desert air lifts the sand up to 9 km (5.6 mi.) above sea level. It floats

across the world and eventually rains down onto your clothes, your hair and, yes, the floor under your bed.

With all that great dirt in and under your bed, it's not surprising you've got dirt eaters down there, too. There are more than a million dust mites in an average bed. You can't see them or hear them, but they're everywhere. Under a microscope, they look like naked crabs with eight legs. Dust mites don't really eat dust; they eat flakes of skin. And they never go hungry. When you walk, you shed tens of thousands of skin flakes each minute. Yum!

Dirt fun

Kids around the world have loved to play in the dirt since the beginning of time. Dirt-bike racing is one of the newer ways.

It started in California as a kid version of motorcycle racing. Kids belong to bike clubs and compete in official races for points and national ranking.

Dirt-bike racing can be a dangerous sport, so bikes and bikers wear protective clothing. Bikes have thick foam pads covering bars, tubes and sharp edges. Bikers wear official racing helmets, goggles, elbow pads, knee pads, laced-up shoes (slip-on shoes slip off and make you fall) and racing gloves. Head-to-toe clothes are a good idea, too.

Bikers race at speeds of up to 32 km/h (20 m.p.h.). Along the way, they have to clear a series of obstacles, such as "cliffs" up to 2 m (6.5 ft.) high or a row of three bumps, sometimes called a whoop-de-doo. When the bumps are close together, some racers fly over all three in one jump called a bunny hop. If the bumps aren't too steep, bikers can pull a wheelie and ride over them on their back wheel. Most racers just take it slowly.

Start your pedals!

You don't need an official track to have fun with your bikes. Get your friends together and make a simple version in the dirt. Use pails of water and shovels to shape some hills and bumps. Keep them low so racers can ride over them safely. Put big cans on the ground for bikers to weave in and out and around.

When you get bored, try a slow bike race. The object is to ride as slowly as possible without ever touching your feet to the ground. The winner is the slowest rider.

Making mud cake

Remember mud pies? This cake recipe doesn't use real mud, but it's just as dark and gooey and tastes much, much better. It looks hard to make because of all the ingredients, but it's as easy as ... mud pie. Try it.

You'll need
- a rectangular cake pan
- shortening
- a large mixing bowl
- 150 mL (2/3 c.) cocoa
- 500 mL (2 c.) flour
- 400 mL (1 2/3 c.) sugar
- 400 mL (1 2/3 c.) water
- 150 mL (2/3 c.) soft butter
- 3 eggs
- 10 mL (2 tsp.) instant coffee
- 7 mL (1 1/2 tsp.) baking soda
- 2 mL (1/2 tsp.) baking powder
- 5 mL (1 tsp.) vanilla extract
- 2 mL (1/2 tsp.) salt
- an electric beater

1 Preheat the oven to 350°F (180°C).

2 Grease the pan with shortening.

3 Put all the ingredients into the bowl.

4 Beat everything together for two minutes.

5 Pour the mixture into the cake pan.

6 Bake for 40 minutes.

To make the cake extra "muddy," spread chocolate fudge icing over the top and decorate with black licorice.

DIRT MATTERS
Get a close-up

Grab a handful of dirt and take a good look. Feel it, smell it, crumble it between your fingers. What do you discover? If you sample dirt from different places, you'll see that each handful is a little different. One handful might feel firm but then squish into slimy paste between your fingers. Another sample might be so dry it almost floats into the air.

Dirt is both organic (made of things that are living or were once living) and inorganic (made of things that have never lived, such as crushed rock). How a handful looks and feels depends on the type of plants and animals in the area, the local weather and the kind of rocks under the soil.

Have you ever seen red or yellow soil? How about blue, brown or black soil? All those colors are there if you look for them. When dirt looks red, there is some iron in the local rocks. When dirt is gray or even blue, there is marshland nearby. If you grab a handful of dirt that is deep brown or black — start planting. You have found terrific growing soil, rich in humus. Humus is the main ingredient in the best top soil. It's made from nature's garbage (rotted leaves, sticks, roots and dead insects) with help from nature's living recyclers (fungi, mold, bacteria and earthworms).

Make the world's greatest dirt

Gardeners know they get the biggest, healthiest plants when they add humus to the top soil. You can make your own humus by starting a mini composter.

The combination of heat, water, bacteria and organic garbage makes a nutritious mix for your garden. Don't worry about creating a big stink. If you follow the directions, there'll be no smell at all.

You'll need
- a clean, empty cardboard milk carton
- waterproof tape, such as duct tape
- scissors
- fruit and vegetable scraps — no fat or meat
- a knife
- a spoon
- garden soil

1 Seal the open end of the carton with tape. Lay the carton on its side.

2 Ask an adult to help you cut a flap on the side big enough to reach inside with a spoon.

3 Cut some food scraps into dime-sized pieces. Spoon a thin layer into the carton.

4 Cover with a thin layer of soil and mix everything together.

5 Each day, stir well and add more scraps and soil until the mix is about 3 cm (1.2 in.) from the top. Set the carton aside.

6 Keep stirring the mix every day, adding a bit of water if it starts to look dry. In a few weeks, you'll have a box of dark, rich humus.

What's in dirt?

Dirt isn't the same all the way through. Try this to find out just what's in the dirt in your own yard or area.

You'll need
- a few handfuls of dirt
- a large jar with a lid
- water

1 Put the dirt into the jar and fill it with water. Screw the lid on tight.

2 Give the jar a good shake and let it sit for a few days. What happens?

When you shake the jar, the dirt settles into layers. Study the layers with a magnifying glass if you have one. How many of these layers can you identify? They should settle in the following order, with gravel at the bottom:

Humus: Dark, moist soil made when food, leaves, sticks, roots and insects die and rot.

Clay: Slimy, slippery soil made of very fine particles smaller than 0.004 mm (0.00016 in.).

Silt: Mud formed from tiny pieces of rock. Its fine grains measure from 0.004 mm (0.00016 in.) to 0.06 mm (0.0024 in.).

Sand: Coarser grains measuring from 0.06 mm (0.0024 in.) to 2.0 mm (0.08 in.).

Gravel: Larger, visible rock particles.

Tired of sand-colored sand?

Sand can be almost any color. The coral-colored sand of Bermuda is made of limestone, coral and shell fragments. The black sand of Hawaii is made from the molten rock of volcanoes, which cooled and was washed to the sea by mountain streams. There is even green sand on the ocean floor — it contains bits of glauconite.

Hawaii's black volcanic sand

GEEZER ROCKS

The world's oldest known rocks are probably in Western Australia. Scientists there have found tiny crystals of zircon sandwiched in sandstone, which they say are 4.4 billion years old.

How rocks become dirt

As you read this, rocks around the world are slowly changing into dirt. This process is called weathering, and you can see signs of it going on all around you.

Rock sculptures are the work of wind or water, rubbing off bits that eventually become dirt. Percé Rock in Quebec has a hole 30 m (100 ft.) wide carved through it by crashing waves. A rushing river created the spectacular Grand Canyon.

A rock carving made by wind and waves

Erode a rock

FUN with Dirt

Make your own Percé Rock. (To save a few years, use ice.) Freeze water in a pie plate. Hold the ice disc under a tap so that the water erodes it and makes a hole. Lift out the ice and look through. Water does the same thing with rock.

Pebbles on a beach are rocks on their way to becoming sand, an important ingredient of dirt. Waves tumble large rocks like clothes in a dryer until they break apart and all the rough edges get worn off.

Cracks break down rocks, too. Rocks expand in the sun's warmth and shrink at night when the temperature drops. Eventually, the rocks crack. Water freezes in the cracks, widening them. Bits of rock fall off and are worn down more by wind and rain.

Plants start to grow in small crevices in the rock and force bits of the rock to crumble off. These tiny bits become the dirt in which other plants grow.

FUN with Dirt Shake it!

Collect some small, rough-edged rocks, put them in a can with a plastic lid and shake 'em up. (You might need some help.) Shake for five minutes, then carefully open the can. Run your finger around the inside. Congratulations! You've just made sand.

Now look at your rocks. Are the edges a bit worn down? Imagine what would happen if these rocks were tumbled around on a beach for thousands of years.

ON THE ROCKS

Some of the dirt in your backyard was probably made by glaciers millions of years ago. Glaciers are thick slabs of slowly moving ice. Long ago, huge glaciers moved over much of North America, gouging and crushing rocks in their path. Wind and water did their work, and microscopic bacteria and plants started to live and die in the rock crevices. Finally, dirt formed. It can take from 100 to 10 000 years to make 2 cm (0.8 in.) of good top soil from crushed rock.

Disappearing dirt

Dirt on the move is called erosion. Erosion changes the way our world looks. Sometimes the results are fabulous landforms created by rivers eroding rock. Sometimes erosion is deadly, causing rock slides, mud slides or floods.

Water is one cause of erosion. Rivers moving through rock and over flat land remove loose rock and soil, called sediment. In swift-flowing water, the sediment stays suspended, like herbs in salad dressing. If the water slows for a river bend or flatter land, the sediment sinks and gets left behind. Sediment buildup in a shipping channel can stop boats from passing.

When water can't flow because it's blocked by sediment, floods occur. Add heavy rain and there may be a disaster. Nine million people died when the Yellow River flooded in China during the nineteenth century.

Wind is another cause of erosion. The incredible dust storms of the 1930s stripped farms of good growing soil and led to a decade of drought called the Dirty Thirties. During those years, the wind blew black clouds of dirt 8 km (5 mi.) high around the prairies and even out to sea. Drifts of sand and silt buried homes and barns. No crops grew.

People cause erosion, too. Land that was once fertile is now desert because settlers cut the trees for homes and fuel. Their animals grazed on what remained of the plants. With nothing to anchor the top soil, it blew away or was washed away. Only drifting dust and sand was left. Deserts are growing across North America and Africa. The Sahara Desert is growing by 78 km^2 (30 sq. mi.) a year.

But it might not be too late to save the disappearing land. Building barriers called jetties to trap sediment can stop river erosion. Planting trees, shrubs and grasses on farm fields can anchor the sand and soil. Crops can be irrigated so that their roots grow deep and hold down the soil. And plowing can be done in ways that hold the soil instead of letting it run off with the rain.

OOPS, THERE GOES ANOTHER SYCAMORE TREE

One day in 1981, Rose Owen of Winter Park, Florida, made a frantic call to the police. Her giant sycamore tree had just been swallowed up by the earth, she said. Soon the police were getting more reports. Half of a swimming pool had sunk into the ground. A whole section of a street had disappeared. What was going on?

It turned out that over millions of years, water had eroded the limestone rock under the town, creating an enormous cavern. Usually, the cavern was flooded with water. But a recent drought had kept the water level low. It couldn't support the top soil — or the town — anymore. The earth started to sink and dragged a big chunk of the town down with it, including Mrs. Owen's sycamore.

Here's mud in your eye

Go outside on a windy day and you're almost sure to find yourself blinking hard. You can't see them, but tiny specks of dirt are everywhere in the air. And — ouch — a big one has just landed in your eye.

Small particles of dirt, smaller than the dust under your bed, are important. Without them, there wouldn't be any rain. Water in the air has to stick onto dust to grow into raindrops.

Beautiful sunsets couldn't happen without dirt either. The sun's light is made up of all the colors of the rainbow. The colors are different wavelengths. Red has the longest wavelength; violet has the shortest. At the end of the day, when the sun is near the horizon, its light must pass through the low layer of dust and air near Earth's surface. The short-wavelength colors such as blue and violet bounce off the dust particles and give a dusky glow to the sky. The longer-wavelength colors such as red pass through the dust. This makes the sun look a brilliant red.

Quicksand!

Sand is always shifting. You may think that quicksand, the shiftiest sand, is the imaginary stuff of adventure movies. Think again. Quicksand is very real and exists across North America.

Dry sand sticks together. Wet sand becomes fluid, like water. If pressure builds under really wet sand — let's say, from an underground stream — it becomes quicksand.

People die in quicksand when they panic and thrash around. If you move quickly in quicksand, it loosens for an instant and then packs even more tightly around you. But you can float on quicksand by lying back and gently moving your arms. Then you can backstroke until you're on solid ground.

GULP!

Sand sculpture, nature's way

Think before you scramble up an enormous sand dune the next time you're at the shore. The dunes look solid, but actually they are so fragile that a single footprint could start their collapse.

Dunes get their start when strong currents and high winds deposit sand from the lake or ocean floor onto the beach. The wind picks up the sand and carries it until the sand hits an obstacle, such as a piece of driftwood or grass. The sand starts to build up. Grass grows and spreads, anchoring roots under the surface. When dunes get really high, windstorms, rain or even people walking can destroy the grass-root anchors. That frees the sand to blow farther inland. The sand can pile up in forests and bury them.

That's why at protected beaches you'll find walkways and sand fences to trap the sand.

Earth moves

The earth beneath your feet may feel steady as a rock, but it's actually in constant motion. That's because the ground we live on — Earth's crust — is not a single, solid piece. It's made up of seven huge "plates" that float like icebergs on the surface. These plates are always moving, sliding over and under each other and even bashing together.

Usually the plates move slowly, about 2.5 cm to 5 cm (1 in. to 2 in.) a year. When two plates move away from each other, they leave a gap between them. Hot liquid rock, called magma, from inside Earth oozes out through the gap. Huge chains of volcanoes may form in this way, often on the ocean floor. Some of these underwater mountains grow until they poke out through the surface of the water, forming an island. Iceland is one such island.

Sometimes a plate gets snagged by another plate. When this happens, enormous pressure builds up, until finally an earthquake releases some of the stress.

Plates can also push together and fold the land upward into mountains. That's usually a slow process. The Himalayan mountains started to grow 25 million years ago and are still growing taller because the plate on which India sits is playing push-shove with the Eurasian plate.

This upward thrusting can lift land from the bottom of the sea to the tops of mountains. Mountain climbers have discovered limestone at the top of Mount Everest. Limestone is made from crushed seashells that once lay on the ocean floor.

Digging deep

Ever try digging to the center of Earth? How far did you get? Probably not very far. Geologists with sophisticated equipment have not even punched through Earth's crust.

The deepest hole so far (in northern Russia) took 20 years to drill and reaches 12 km (7.5 mi.) into the crust. But scientists may soon hit Earth's second layer, the mantle, by drilling through the ocean floor, where the crust is thinnest. They will use a drill pipe 25 times the height of the Empire State Building!

If you could slice through Earth as if it were an apple, you would see this:

Crust   5–40 km
            (3–25 mi.)

Mantle 2885 km
            (1793 mi.)

Outer   2270 km
core   (1410 mi.)

Inner   1216 km
core   (756 mi.)

1. Crust: From the top of the mountains to the bottom of the seabed, the crust is at most 70 km (44 mi.) thick. It floats on top of the mantle. It's made up of
- top soil, where most plants and animals live
- subsoil, which is composed of mineral particles
- bedrock, where oil and gas are found

2. Mantle: The top layer is hot rock, some of which is liquid magma. When magma erupts through a volcano, it's called lava.

3. Core: The liquid outer core and solid inner core are made mainly of iron and some nickel, silicon and sulfur. Geologists think the temperature at the center of Earth is 6000°C (10 800°F).

FUN with Dirt

What's the snag?

To see how earthquakes happen, wrap sandpaper around two blocks of wood. Ask an adult to help nail on the sandpaper. Press the blocks together, then try to slide one forward as you pull the other back. Like rocks on the edges of Earth's giant plates, the sandpaper keeps the blocks from sliding. When the force of your pushing becomes too strong, the blocks jerk past each other, just like the movement of plates in an earthquake.

BURIED!
Clues to the past

It's spring, and you're helping to put in the garden. Your shovel hits something hard. You dig it up. It looks like a piece of a flowerpot. You show it to your parents and they tell you it's probably just junk.

But check it out anyway. You'd be amazed at what you might find in your own backyard. In 1989, a team of archaeologists carefully excavated the backyard of a Toronto home because a young girl had dug up a thousand-year-old piece of pottery there. It turned out the girl's find was part of an ancient aboriginal pottery works.

How does stuff from past civilizations get buried? Let's imagine what might have happened to that aboriginal village. Maybe the people were forced to abandon their homes because of fire, drought or war. Eventually, the homes rotted and were covered by dirt and then by forests.

Over the centuries, people used the land for different things. First the same piece of land could have been the home of First Nations peoples, then a settlement for European pioneers, then industrial land and finally a modern apartment development with parks. Every time the land is used for something else, the old stuff is built over or covered up.

Archaeologists look for clues to buried civilizations. Mounds of dirt can be signs that something is buried underneath. Sometimes ancient books give the locations of places that have long since been covered over.

Using such clues, archaeologists begin digging. First they divide the area into a grid of small numbered squares. They carefully dig up each square, using small trowels

and sometimes even teaspoons and toothbrushes so they don't break anything valuable. They remove the top soil — usually about 30 cm (12 in.) deep — and sift it. Any objects they find are labeled and cataloged.

Sometimes archaeologists coat an item in plaster so it won't break apart when it is moved.

Each "strata," or layer of earth, reveals secrets from a different time in the past. You can see strata in your bedroom when you dig through the piles of clothes and toys in your cupboard. Start at the top of the pile for today's clothes and games. Keep digging and you may reach the clothes and toys you received for last year's birthday buried at the bottom. The deeper down you dig, the farther back in time you go. The same thing happens at an archaeological dig.

Once the objects are found, the archaeologists have to figure out how old they are. They piece together bits of pottery, called potsherds, and try to remake bowls and cups. Sometimes they try to reconstruct entire buildings and communities from bits and pieces. Archaeologists put our past together like a puzzle with most of the pieces missing.

Dirt detectives!

Tomb of Zachariah, Jerusalem

In the past, archaeologists were lucky to stumble on a valuable find, such as a long-buried tomb that hadn't been vandalized. They might circle an area and stick long steel rods into the ground. If they hit metal, it meant something was there — but what? After a lot of digging, they might discover an empty tomb. Now archaeologists use machines similar to underground radar to find tombs. Then they dig a hole and lower an upside-down periscope. This allows them to look around and see if the tomb is worth uncovering.

Archaeologists also use airplanes outfitted with cameras to search out new sites. When crops are planted over ruins, they do not grow as tall as other crops. The aerial photos show these "crop marks."

Garbage under your feet

Imagine that the garbage truck didn't arrive for an entire year. You had to pile your garbage in the yard or street. By the end of the year, each person in your house would have contributed 500 kg (1102 lbs.) of garbage — an elephant's weight — to your waste pile. That's a mega-problem.

Most towns truck garbage to vacant land, dump it in huge holes and bury it under dirt. Eventually, this "landfill site" builds into a mountain and is landscaped with trees and grass. Some towns even turn old landfill sites into ski hills in winter.

That sounds pretty good, but there are problems with landfill sites. People throw hazardous household wastes into the trash without realizing they may be poisoning the environment. When bleach and ammonia mix, they can explode and create deadly gases. Chemicals from medicines, pesticides and oven cleaners can seep into water flowing deep underground and poison wells and water supplies. And besides the dangers of burying waste, the world is running out of landfill sites.

The news is not all glum. You can help by recycling paper, plastics and cans. Better yet, stop using as much paper and reuse your plastic bags. Start a compost heap (see page 13). Everyone has to do something to cut down on garbage. Industry is swapping wastes — what one company might throw out, another could use as a raw material. And more communities have curbside recycling programs.

WHY DO DOGS BURY BONES?

So that other dogs and animals won't get them. And maybe because the cooler temperatures underground help preserve any meat on the bones. Burying a bone is like putting it in the refrigerator.

Buried treasure?

There's a mysterious shaft, called the Money Pit, on Oak Island, Nova Scotia, that's caused a whole lot of trouble over the past 200 years. Some folks think pirates' treasure is buried at its bottom, but there's no way of knowing. People have spent millions trying to find the treasure and have come away empty-handed. Six men have died. Whenever someone gets close to the bottom of the shaft, things go wrong ...

It all began in 1795, when a Nova Scotia farmer named Daniel McGinnis found a clearing in the middle of a red oak forest. There'd been rumors for years that pirates used to land on Oak Island and hide their bounty. And so, when Daniel saw a clearing smack in the middle of the dense forest and then noticed a patch of sunken land and some odd carvings on a tree trunk, he was sure he'd stumbled on the hiding place.

He raced to find friends and they started digging. They eased up a layer of stones and found themselves staring into a shallow shaft. There was only one reason for it to be there — someone had buried something: treasure!

They climbed in and kept digging. They hit a platform of rotted logs. They broke it apart and continued digging. Whenever they thought they'd struck gold — wham! — they'd hit wood. Every 3 m (10 ft.) it was the same thing.

At 27 m (89 ft.) down, there was a layer of charcoal, putty and coconut fiber. What was a coconut doing down a shaft? Then their shovels hit rock. They discovered a stone etched with odd symbols. Could this be a secret code? They pried up the stone, and suddenly water started pouring into the shaft. As they scrambled out, they poked with their shovels and felt something hard — like a chest — a bit farther down. But they never reached it. By morning, the shaft was full of seawater.

Nobody could figure out how to drain the shaft, so the Money Pit lay untouched for another 46 years. New fortune hunters came along and used a drill. It pulled up small pieces of metal. Still, not a doubloon or a ruby was found. But the mystery of the flooding shaft was solved. Whoever dug the shaft booby-trapped it by digging two flood tunnels from the shaft to the ocean. At high tide, the water poured in at 4500 L (1200 U.S gal.) a minute! The tricks didn't stop there. The crafty pirates probably dug tunnels that sloped upward from the main shaft. The treasure might be hidden in them. One thing is clear — somebody went to a lot of trouble to hide something.

Bounty seekers have dug up plenty of clues, such as china, brass and a pair of 300-year-old Spanish scissors. There have been so many digs that the original Money Pit has caved in. That won't stop people searching. But for now, the treasure of Oak Island remains buried.

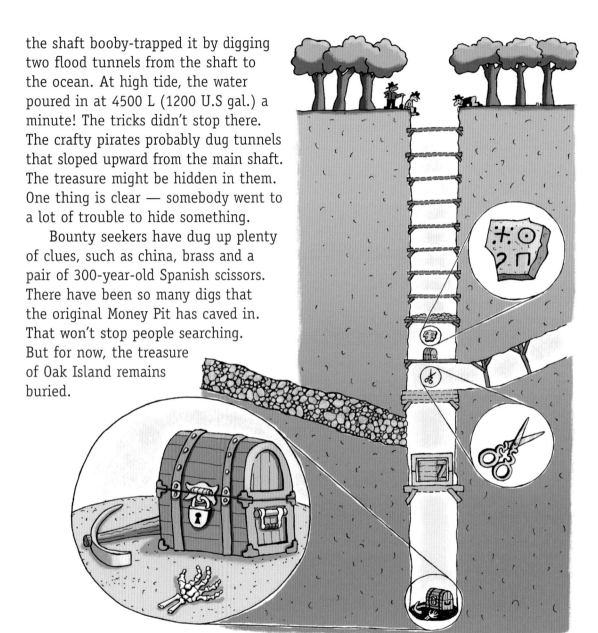

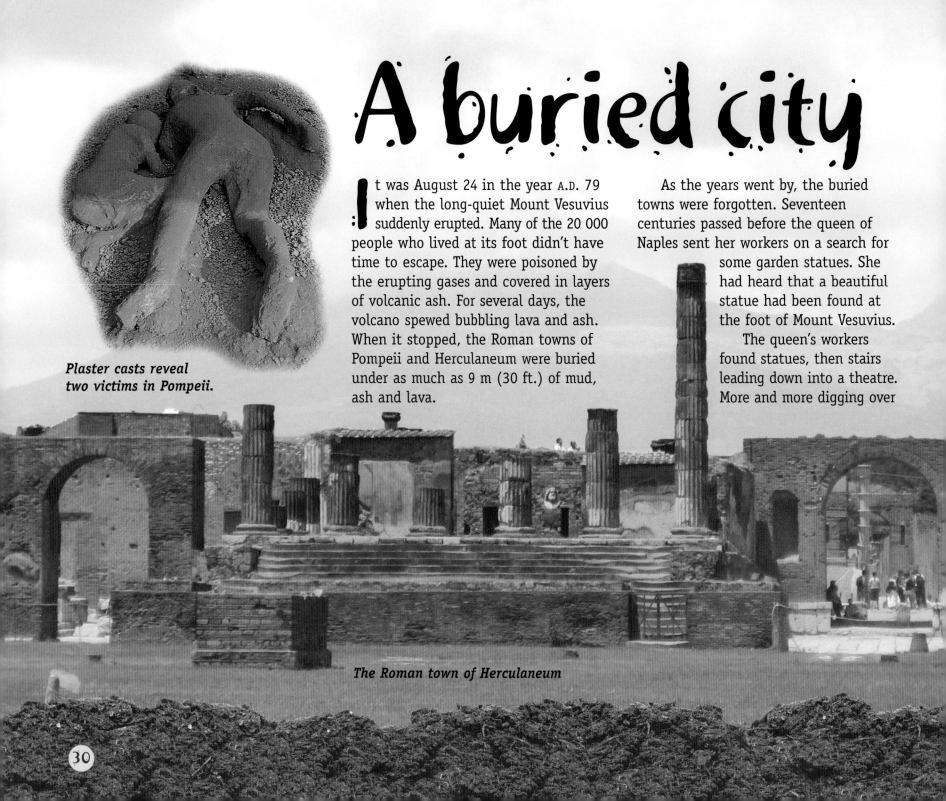

A buried city

It was August 24 in the year A.D. 79 when the long-quiet Mount Vesuvius suddenly erupted. Many of the 20 000 people who lived at its foot didn't have time to escape. They were poisoned by the erupting gases and covered in layers of volcanic ash. For several days, the volcano spewed bubbling lava and ash. When it stopped, the Roman towns of Pompeii and Herculaneum were buried under as much as 9 m (30 ft.) of mud, ash and lava.

As the years went by, the buried towns were forgotten. Seventeen centuries passed before the queen of Naples sent her workers on a search for some garden statues. She had heard that a beautiful statue had been found at the foot of Mount Vesuvius.

The queen's workers found statues, then stairs leading down into a theatre. More and more digging over

Plaster casts reveal two victims in Pompeii.

The Roman town of Herculaneum

hundreds of years uncovered an entire, perfectly preserved city.

Today if you visit Pompeii, you'll see everything exactly as it was that long-ago August day when Vesuvius erupted. A pig roasts on a fireplace, dogs are tied up at posts, and people are huddled in corners with their hands protecting their faces from the deadly fumes. There are even loaves of bread in an oven. The life of a town has been preserved in time.

When the site of Pompeii was discovered in Italy, all remains of the people and animals had rotted away. Only holes in the compacted ash showed where they had once been. Then archaeologist Giuseppe Fiorelli had a brilliant idea. He poured plaster into the holes in the lava. When the plaster dried, he had perfect plaster casts of the people. Even the expressions on their faces had been captured. Look at them and you can see how terrifying the volcanic eruption must have been.

...And a buried army

In 1974, archaeologists unearthed an entire Chinese army. They were digging on a peasant's farm near the city of Xi'an when they uncovered plaster, woven mats and wooden beams. They had found the tomb of the first emperor of China, Qin Shi Huangdi, who died in 210 B.C. They uncovered 7000 life-sized, hollow clay soldiers standing in long corridors and rooms, guarding their emperor as he passed into the "next life."

The clay army was magnificent. Each statue was beautifully carved and had a different expression on its face. The soldiers wore full costumes and carried weapons. They were accompanied by clay horses and chariots.

Fossils in the mud

ANCIENT INSECT

The oldest fossilized insect in the world was found embedded in mudstone on the north shore of the Gaspé Peninsula in Quebec. This relative of the pesky silverfish lived 390 million years ago.

Mud is more than a gushy mushy mixture of soil and water that makes gloopy sounds when you walk in it. It serves a useful purpose — it helps to preserve plants and animals that lived millions of years ago. Mud is often the first step in the creation of a fossil.

Fossils are the preserved remains of plants and animals. Sometimes an entire animal — skin, teeth and bones — gets fossilized. Whole ancient animals have been found in hardened mud and tar pits. But usually only parts of the plant or animal are fossilized.

Here's what happens. When the plant or animal dies, it gets buried in sand or mud. The soft parts rot, leaving only the shells or bones. Water flows in and around the leftover bits and seeps into tiny holes in shell or bone. When the water dries up, minerals are left behind. These minerals change the shell or bone into rock.

Fossils are everywhere, but you have to keep your eyes open. The next time you walk along a rocky shore, pick up the rocks and look at them closely. Or look at roadside rocks that have been blasted to make way for a highway. If you are lucky, you may even find fossils of dinosaur footprints from millions of years ago.

Making tracks

Imagine this: A group of prehistoric creatures stop for a drink by a river and leave footprints in the muddy bank. Later, a rain of volcanic ash buries the footprints. Eventually, the mud hardens into rock.

A million years later, the preserved footprints — called trace fossils — will give scientists information about the size and habits of the animals that left their traces in the ancient mud. Here's how you can preserve your own muddy footprints.

You'll need
- a muddy place on a dry day (your trace fossil has to dry fast!)
- waterproof tape, such as duct tape
- a long strip of cardboard at least 5 cm (2 in.) wide
- 250 mL (1 c.) water
- 500 mL (2 c.) plaster of Paris
- a clean old tin can
- a stick

1 Make a clear footprint in the mud.

2 Tape the edges of the cardboard together in an oval shape large enough to surround your footprint.

3 Press this cardboard collar into the mud around your print to form a mold.

4 Use the stick to mix the water and plaster of Paris in the tin can until it is as thick as pancake batter.

5 Pour the wet plaster of Paris into your mold. It should be about 2.5 cm (1 in.) thick.

6 Let it dry. This takes about half a day.

7 Lift the cardboard and plaster cast. Carefully wipe away any dirt.
You can also make casts of any animal tracks you find.

Dirt homes

Under your feet lies another world, where moles tunnel, owls burrow, ants excavate, earthworms devour and brown rats race around in mazes. Ready to take a peek and see what lurks below?

• Charles Darwin used to play classical music to his worms. They ate during high notes and scurried underground on low ones. What do you think they'd do if they heard rap music? For more about the amazing earthworm, turn the page.

• Brown rats are smart. Once they discover poison bait, they stay away — even if it's disguised or moved. They scurry under the cover of dirt, leaves or snow to avoid predators, such as cats and birds.

• Some ants have "ant cows." These are really aphids, little insects that suck the juice out of plants to make sugar water (below). The ants protect the aphids and even tend their eggs underground. What do the ants get out of it? You guessed it — a sweet drink they "milk" from their "cows."

A VERY LONG NAP

The African lungfish usually lives in the muddy bottoms of swamps and lakes. It snuggles in the soft mud and comes up to the surface for air. But during droughts, the lungfish folds up its 2 m (6.5 ft.) long body, coats itself with mucus and goes into a deep sleep called estivation (hibernation during the hot season). The mud around the fish dries and bakes into a hard shell. Amazingly, the lungfish can exist inside this mud coffin without food and water for four years. When the rains start, the mud softens and the lungfish wakes up.

• The incredible digging mole can eat 40 000 insects and worms each year.

• Burrowing owls usually live in desert-like places and move into abandoned burrows. They have two sets of eyelids that blink like windshield wipers to keep dirt from their eyes.

Plants' best friend

Your garden would be a disaster without earthworms. They turn rotting plants and animals into rich fertilizer. And as they burrow through the soil, they create spaces for air and water to flow.

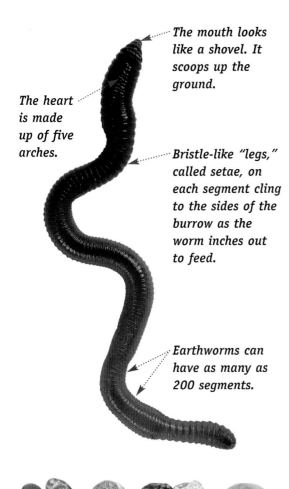

The mouth looks like a shovel. It scoops up the ground.

The heart is made up of five arches.

Bristle-like "legs," called setae, on each segment cling to the sides of the burrow as the worm inches out to feed.

Earthworms can have as many as 200 segments.

LOOOOOONG!

The longest earthworm in the world measured 6.7 m (22 ft.) and was found in South Africa.

True or false?

Think you know earthworms? Try this quiz. (Answers are on page 46.)

1. Each earthworm is both male and female and can have babies without ever meeting another worm.

2. Earthworms breathe through special holes near their tails.

3. A single hectare of land can be home to 23 000 earthworms. (A single acre is home to 56 800 earthworms.)

4. If you cut an earthworm in half, it will grow a new head and tail.

5. Earthworms hibernate in the winter.

6. Some earthworms grow very long and make gurgling noises when they move.

7. People once believed that earthworms fell from the sky when it rained.

8. Earthworms can eat their weight in soil in a day.

9. An earthworm is tough to pull out of its burrow because it glues itself to the soil.

SNEAK UP ON A WORM

Worms come out at night, but they disappear if you go close to them with a flashlight. Try covering your light with red cellophane — worms can't see red light. And walk softly — worms feel vibrations and will retreat into their burrows.

Tunnels and towers

Tunneling comes naturally to some animals. But when people build tunnels in the ground, they have to do a lot of planning. Engineers design the tunnels. Geologists dig into the soil and rock to take samples and decide the best places and the best ways to dig. Then the digging begins.

Workers dig a shaft into the ground. All the equipment and workers enter the tunnel through this shaft. Two crews of tunnel builders dig in opposite directions to speed up the work.

Bulldozers and shovels are used to dig out the mud. Often, large tunnels are "shield driven." This means a large circular piece of metal is shoved through the ground by hydraulic jacks. Little railway cars are loaded with the rocks and debris that must be removed from the tunnel.

Workers support the sides and top of the tunnel with pieces of curved steel called ribs. To prevent cave-ins, sometimes the tunnel is coated with a layer of concrete, or long bolts are drilled through the roof to hold it firmly to the surrounding rock.

Top digs

• The longest continuous subway tunnel is in Moscow. It runs for about 31 km (19 mi.).

• To build the 50 km (31 mi.) Channel Tunnel (or "Chunnel") linking Britain and France, workers removed 8 000 000 m³ (282 500 000 cu. ft.) of soil — three times the volume of the Great Pyramid in Egypt.

• The tallest, widest tunnel — 23 m (75.5 ft.) wide and 17 m (56 ft.) high — is in Yerba Buena Island, San Francisco. More than 80 million cars, trucks and buses move through this two-level tunnel every year.

Watch out below!

The Leaning Tower of Pisa in Italy used to lean farther to one side every year. Architects thought it might topple one day.

Over the years, many attempts were made to fix the lean, but all failed. Then, in 1999, engineers began slowly removing soil from the high side. It worked! The tower began to straighten. But engineers will only straighten it 10 percent — that should stabilize it for hundreds of years, while keeping its unique lean.

The probable reason for the lean is that the builders in 1174 didn't know much about dirt. They built the tower on sandy soil that was softer on one side than the other. So the tower soon started to sink lower and lower on the softer side.

Builders today would bore into the soil at different depths and in different places, then study the samples to decide how much weight the soil could hold. Rock, clay and sand support different weights. They might build a wide foundation to spread the weight of a tower built on uneven ground.

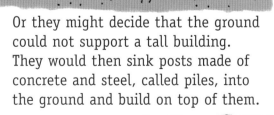

Or they might decide that the ground could not support a tall building. They would then sink posts made of concrete and steel, called piles, into the ground and build on top of them.

A cathedral termite mound

More dirt homes

When people around the world make homes for themselves, they look for materials that are cheap and handy. You can't get much cheaper or handier than mud.

Building with dirt is an idea people have borrowed from animals. Termites in Africa and Australia dot the flatlands with volcano-shaped mud homes, some as tall as barns. Some birds use mud to cement twigs

A beaver dam packed with mud

mix mud with grass and straw. This material, called adobe, can be spread over a twig frame while it's still wet or can be patted into shapes and baked in the sun until it's hard. Adobe homes more than 10 000 years old have been discovered in the Middle East.

Today we use a modern version of adobe: brick. A brick house is weather-tight and impervious to rain and snow. And no matter how hard the big bad wolf huffs and puffs, he's out of luck.

and leaves together for sturdy nests, and beavers pack their dams with mud for waterproofing and weatherproofing.

Keeping warm in winter and cool in summer leads some people to dig right into the sides of hills to make their homes. The earth helps insulate the house. Other people shovel a layer of dirt onto their roofs and plant grass in it. Grass is a good roofing material — it keeps out the rain and keeps the inside temperature even. How do these home owners stop the roof from growing? Why, they get a goat, of course.

Africans and Native Americans from the southern United States and Central America use dirt for building. They

Easy-peasy plants

Have you ever eaten a tomato picked straight off the vine or chased a butterfly through a meadow? That's only for country kids, right? No way. If you have dirt, you can have wild gardens or pots of flowers or veggies anywhere — even in the city. Here are three fun ways to bring some great greenery into your life.

Carefree cactus

A cactus garden is probably the easiest garden to tend. Cactuses are used to being ignored! Fill a shallow clay pot with sandy soil. (You might even have a clay pot you made at camp sitting around.) Plant different kinds of cactus — the hairy kind is called old man cactus, the hedge cactus looks like a cucumber, and the golden ball cactus looks like its name. Put your pot in a sunny window. And don't overwater!

In the spring and summer, water only when the top 2.5 cm (1 in.) of soil is dry. In the winter, put it in a cool, sunny place and water every two months. How easy is that?

Go wild

Grow a no-fuss weed garden by collecting floating seeds from the air or ground. Use an old milk carton or can (poke a few holes in the bottom for drainage), add some potting soil, then sprinkle your seeds on top. Cover the seeds with a layer of soil and water well. You may discover some beautiful weeds.

Yellow!

If you have a yard, plant sunflower seeds in a hot, sunny place. You'll not only attract birds, but you'll also have some great-tasting seeds to roast at the end of the summer. (Give seeds to all your friends and see who ends up with the tallest sunflower.)

Rain forest in a bottle

FUN with Dirt

Rain forests thrive on heat and rain. To make a miniature version, you'll need a large glass bottle with a wide mouth, or a fish tank and a piece of glass that covers the top. Put a layer of clean gravel and some charcoal (from your fireplace or campfire) on the bottom, cover with a rich layer of compost or top soil, and plant three or four small tropical plants, such as mosses, ferns, pitcher plants or impatiens. (Tiny varieties are available at some garden centers.) Water well, put on the lid and place your mini rain forest in a sunny spot. And here's the surprise — you won't have to water again for a couple of months. Can you figure out why? (See page 46.)

Growing naturally

When you nibble a carrot or munch on an apple, the last thing you worry about are the chemicals you might be eating. Farmers use chemicals on their crops to get rid of unwanted bugs and to make the produce grow bigger and look better. Producers may coat their fruits and vegetables with chemicals so they stay fresher longer. Apples and cucumbers aren't shiny when they come off the tree or vine — that's a wax you're eating!

Some people want food grown naturally — without any chemicals. And they are willing to pay the price. Organic food costs more because it's more expensive to produce and sell. And the fruits and vegetables do not always look perfect. But people who buy organic food believe it tastes better and

is healthier for them and for the planet.

So how do farmers grow organically? They use compost and manure for fertilizer instead of chemicals. They get rid of bugs with other bugs. (A bug that eats one crop may be a tasty treat for another bug.) Farmers can also use flowers to control bugs. For example, the smell of marigolds is so obnoxious to some bugs and small animals that they leave nearby crops alone. And farmers make sure the ground is kept rich in minerals and nutrients by moving the crops around from season to season. Peas and beans put minerals into the soil, but wheat and barley gobble minerals up.

As organic food becomes more and more available in stores, prices may drop and more people will be able to try it.

Grow a hideaway

Next time you need a place to get away from it all, why not grow it? In about two months, you can grow a leafy and edible house with pole beans. And if you buy scarlet runner bean seeds, which blossom into brilliant red flowers, you might attract hummingbirds.

You'll need
- a large garden spot with good soil
- 6 poles or pieces of doweling, each 2 m (6.5 ft.) long
- strong string
- pole bean seeds

1 Make a tepee shape with the poles. Push the ends of the poles into the ground. Get a friend to help you tie the tops together with strong string.

2 Tie string between each pole so the bean vines can grab onto something. Don't forget to leave a hole so you can get into your hideaway.

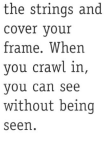

3 Plant three or four seeds at the base of each pole. Cover them with about 2.5 cm (1 in.) of dirt.

4 Water the seeds and plants frequently. The vines will grow along the strings and cover your frame. When you crawl in, you can see without being seen.

Answers

"Plants' best friend" (page 37)

1. False. Earthworms have male and female organs, but they must mate with another earthworm to reproduce. First they exchange sperm, then each worm secretes a slime ring around its body and the fertilized egg. Each parent slithers out of the slime, which hardens into an egg case. In 30 to 100 days, a baby earthworm emerges.

2. False. Earthworms breathe through their skins. They must stay moist or they die.

3. True. And more in lush garden soil.

4. False. Most scientists say that if a worm is cut at certain segments, the head section might grow a new tail, but the tail part cannot grow a new head.

5. True. They dig below the frost line and spend a dozy winter.

6. True. In Australia, earthworms 4 m (13 ft.) long slither underground and make sounds like giant bathtubs draining.

7. True. After a heavy rain, burrows fill with water and the worms slither up to the surface. In the old days, people just saw the wet worms and drew the wrong conclusion.

8. True. They digest the organic matter (rotting plants and animals) and release the rest.

9. False. It's the setae that hold tight to burrow walls.

"Rain forest in a bottle" (page 43)

You have created a mini water cycle in the bottle. The roots draw moisture up, and the leaves send it out into the air. It collects on the lid and "rains" back down on the plants.

Glossary

Archaeologist: a scientist who studies how people lived in the past.

Bacteria: microscopic organisms. Some cause disease; others cause decay. Some are helpful, such as bacteria used to make yogurt.

Emulsifier: a substance that causes ingredients to mix together without separating. For example, soap is an emulsifier that makes oil and water molecules mix.

Estivation: hibernation during an area's hot season.

Erosion: the changing of riverbanks, mountains and other landforms by natural forces, such as wind and water.

Geologist: a scientist who studies the rocks that make up Earth's crust.

Humus: an ingredient of soil made from decayed plants and animals.

Magma: liquid rock under Earth's crust.

Minerals: the basic ingredients of rocks.

Molecules: the tiny building blocks of all things.

Organic food: food grown without chemical fertilizers or pest killers.

Parasite: a plant or animal that lives on another plant or animal to survive.

Sediment: solids that have been deposited by wind, water or glaciers.

Top soil: the top layer of soil that has the nutrients plants need for growing.

Weathering: the natural wearing down of rocks into dirt.

Index